2022-2026 Five Year Planner

Emergency Information

If found, please return to:

Phone: Email:

In case of emergency please contact:

Name: Relationship:

Phone:

Address: City: State:

Email:

Name: Relationship:

Phone:

Address: City: State:

Email:

Primary Care Provider:

Name of Practice:

Phone:

Address: City: State:

Email:

Dentist:

Name of Practice:

Phone:

Address: City: State:

Email:

Other Medical Provider:

Name of Practice:

Phone:

Address: City: State:

Email:

Allergies:

Blood type:

Conditions/Disability:

Medications:

Other:

Holidays

	2022	2023	2024	2025	2026
New Year's Day	Sat, 1/1	Sun, 1/1	Mon, 1/1	Wed, 1/1	Thurs, 1/1
Martin Luther King Day	Mon, 1/17	Mon, 1/16	Mon, 1/15	Mon, 1/20	Mon, 1/19
Lunar New Year	Tues, 2/1	Sun, 1/22	Mon, 1/15	Wed, 2/29	Tues, 2/17
Valentine's Day	Mon, 2/14	Tues, 2/14	Wed, 2/14	Fri, 2/14	Sat, 2/14
President's Day	Mon, 2/21	Mon, 2/20	Mon, 2/19	Mon, 2/17	Mon, 2/16
Mardi Gras	Tues, 3/1	Tues, 2/21	Tues, 2/13	Tues, 3/4	Tues, 2/17
International Women's Day	Sun, 3/8	Wed, 3/8	Fri, 3/8	Sat, 3/8	Sun, 3/8
Daylight Savings	Sun, 3/13	Sun, 3/12	Sun, 3/10	Sun, 3/9	Sun, 3/8
St. Patrick's Day	Thurs, 3/17	Fri, 3/17	Sun, 3/17	Mon, 3/17	Tues, 3/17
Easter	Sun, 4/17	Sun, 4/9	Sun, 3/31	Sun, 4/20	Sun, 4/5
Passover	Fri, 4/15-4/23	Wed, 4/5-4/13	Mon, 4/22-4/30	Sat, 4/12- 4/20	Wed, 4/1- 4/9
Earth Day	Fri, 4/22	Sat, 4/22	Mon, 4/22	Tues, 4/22	Wed, 4/22
Mother's Day	Sun, 5/8	Sun, 5/14	Sun, 5/12	Sun, 5/11	Sun, 5/10
Memorial Day	Mon, 5/30	Mon, 5/29	Mon 5/27	Mon, 5/26	Mon, 5/25
Father's Day	Sun, 6/1	Sun, 6/18	Sun, 6/16	Sun, 6/15	Sun, 6/21
Juneteenth	Fri, 6/19	Mon, 6/19	Wed 6/19	Tues 6/19	Fri 6/19
Independence Day	Mon, 7/4	Tues, 7/4	Thurs, 7/4	Fri, 7/4	Sat, 7/4
Labor Day	Mon, 9/5	Mon, 9/4	Mon, 9/2	Mon, 9/1	Mon, 9/7
Rosh Hashanah	Sun, 9/25-9/27	Fri, 9/15-9/17	Wed, 10/2-10/4	Mon, 9/22- 9/24	Fri, 9/11- 9/13
Yom Kippur	Tues, 10/4	Sun, 9/24	Fri, 11/11	Wed, 10/1	Sun, 9/20
Diwali	Mon, 10/24	Sun, 11/12	Thurs 10/31	Tues, 10/21	Sun, 11/8
Columbus Day	Mon, 10/10	Mon, 10/9	Mon, 10/14	Mon, 10/13	Mon, 10/12
Daylight Savings	Sun, 11/6	Sun, 11/5	Sun, 11/3	Sun, 11/2	Sun, 11/1
Veterans Day	Fri, 11/11	Sat, 11/11 (Obs. 11/10)	Mon, 11/11	Tues, 11/11	Wed, 11/11
Halloween	Mon, 10/31	Tues, 10/31	Thurs, 10/31	Fri, 10/31	Sat, 10/31
Thanksgiving	Thurs, 11/24	Thurs, 11/23	Thur, 11/28	Thurs, 11/27	Thurs, 11/26
Christmas Day	Sun, 12/25	Mon, 12/25	Wed, 12/25	Thurs, 12/25	Fri, 12/25
New Years Eve	Sat, 12/31	Sun, 12/31	Tues, 12/31	Wed, 12/31	Thurs, 12/31

Birthdays & Important Dates

January

February

March

April

May

June

Birthdays & Important Dates

July

August

September

October

November

December

2021

January

SUN	MON	TUE	WED	THU	FRI	SAT
					1	2
3	4	5	6	7	8	9
10	11	12	13	14	15	16
17	18	19	20	21	22	23
24	25	26	27	28	29	30
31						

February

SUN	MON	TUE	WED	THU	FRI	SAT
	1	2	3	4	5	6
7	8	9	10	11	12	13
14	15	16	17	18	19	20
21	22	23	24	25	26	27
28						

March

SUN	MON	TUE	WED	THU	FRI	SAT
	1	2	3	4	5	6
7	8	9	10	11	12	13
14	15	16	17	18	19	20
21	22	23	24	25	26	27
28	29	30	31			

April

SUN	MON	TUE	WED	THU	FRI	SAT
				1	2	3
4	5	6	7	8	9	10
11	12	13	14	15	16	17
18	19	20	21	22	23	24
25	26	27	28	29	30	

May

SUN	MON	TUE	WED	THU	FRI	SAT
						1
2	3	4	5	6	7	8
9	10	11	12	13	14	15
16	17	18	19	20	21	22
23	24	25	26	27	28	29
30	31					

June

SUN	MON	TUE	WED	THU	FRI	SAT
		1	2	3	4	5
6	7	8	9	10	11	12
13	14	15	16	17	18	19
20	21	22	23	24	25	26
27	28	29	30			

July

SUN	MON	TUE	WED	THU	FRI	SAT
				1	2	3
4	5	6	7	8	9	10
11	12	13	14	15	16	17
18	19	20	21	22	23	24
25	26	27	28	29	30	31

August

SUN	MON	TUE	WED	THU	FRI	SAT
1	2	3	4	5	6	7
8	9	10	11	12	13	14
15	16	17	18	19	20	21
22	23	24	25	26	27	28
29	30	31				

September

SUN	MON	TUE	WED	THU	FRI	SAT
			1	2	3	4
5	6	7	8	9	10	11
12	13	14	15	16	17	18
19	20	21	22	23	24	25
26	27	28	29	30		

October

SUN	MON	TUE	WED	THU	FRI	SAT
					1	2
3	4	5	6	7	8	9
10	11	12	13	14	15	16
17	18	19	20	21	22	23
24	25	26	27	28	29	30
31						

November

SUN	MON	TUE	WED	THU	FRI	SAT
	1	2	3	4	5	6
7	8	9	10	11	12	13
14	15	16	17	18	19	20
21	22	23	24	25	26	27
28	29	30				

December

SUN	MON	TUE	WED	THU	FRI	SAT
			1	2	3	4
5	6	7	8	9	10	11
12	13	14	15	16	17	18
19	20	21	22	23	24	25
26	27	28	29	30	31	

2022

January

SUN	MON	TUE	WED	THU	FRI	SAT
						1
2	3	4	5	6	7	8
9	10	11	12	13	14	15
16	17	18	19	20	21	22
23	24	25	26	27	28	29
30	31					

February

SUN	MON	TUE	WED	THU	FRI	SAT
		1	2	3	4	5
6	7	8	9	10	11	12
13	14	15	16	17	18	19
20	21	22	23	24	25	26
27	28					

March

SUN	MON	TUE	WED	THU	FRI	SAT
		1	2	3	4	5
6	7	8	9	10	11	12
13	14	15	16	17	18	19
20	21	22	23	24	25	26
27	28	29	30	31		

April

SUN	MON	TUE	WED	THU	FRI	SAT
					1	2
3	4	5	6	7	8	9
10	11	12	13	14	15	16
17	18	19	20	21	22	23
24	25	26	27	28	29	30

May

SUN	MON	TUE	WED	THU	FRI	SAT
1	2	3	4	5	6	7
8	9	10	11	12	13	14
15	16	17	18	19	20	21
22	23	24	25	26	27	28
29	30	31				

June

SUN	MON	TUE	WED	THU	FRI	SAT
			1	2	3	4
5	6	7	8	9	10	11
12	13	14	15	16	17	18
19	20	21	22	23	24	25
26	27	28	29	30		

July

SUN	MON	TUE	WED	THU	FRI	SAT
					1	2
3	4	5	6	7	8	9
10	11	12	13	14	15	16
17	18	19	20	21	22	23
24	25	26	27	28	29	30
31						

August

SUN	MON	TUE	WED	THU	FRI	SAT
	1	2	3	4	5	6
7	8	9	10	11	12	13
14	15	16	17	18	19	20
21	22	23	24	25	26	27
28	29	30	31			

September

SUN	MON	TUE	WED	THU	FRI	SAT
				1	2	3
4	5	6	7	8	9	10
11	12	13	14	15	16	17
18	19	20	21	22	23	24
25	26	27	28	29	30	

October

SUN	MON	TUE	WED	THU	FRI	SAT
						1
2	3	4	5	6	7	8
9	10	11	12	13	14	15
16	17	18	19	20	21	22
23	24	25	26	27	28	29
30	31					

November

SUN	MON	TUE	WED	THU	FRI	SAT
		1	2	3	4	5
6	7	8	9	10	11	12
13	14	15	16	17	18	19
20	21	22	23	24	25	26
27	28	29	30			

December

SUN	MON	TUE	WED	THU	FRI	SAT
				1	2	3
4	5	6	7	8	9	10
11	12	13	14	15	16	17
18	19	20	21	22	23	24
25	26	27	28	29	30	31

2023

January

SUN	MON	TUE	WED	THU	FRI	SAT
1	2	3	4	5	6	7
8	9	10	11	12	13	14
15	16	17	18	19	20	21
22	23	24	25	26	27	28
29	30	31				

February

SUN	MON	TUE	WED	THU	FRI	SAT
			1	2	3	4
5	6	7	8	9	10	11
12	13	14	15	16	17	18
19	20	21	22	23	24	25
26	27	28				

March

SUN	MON	TUE	WED	THU	FRI	SAT
			1	2	3	4
5	6	7	8	9	10	11
12	13	14	15	16	17	18
19	20	21	22	23	24	25
26	27	28	29	30	31	

April

SUN	MON	TUE	WED	THU	FRI	SAT
						1
2	3	4	5	6	7	8
9	10	11	12	13	14	15
16	17	18	19	20	21	22
23	24	25	26	27	28	29
30						

May

SUN	MON	TUE	WED	THU	FRI	SAT
	1	2	3	4	5	6
7	8	9	10	11	12	13
14	15	16	17	18	19	20
21	22	23	24	25	26	27
28	29	30	31			

June

SUN	MON	TUE	WED	THU	FRI	SAT
				1	2	3
4	5	6	7	8	9	10
11	12	13	14	15	16	17
18	19	20	21	22	23	24
25	26	27	28	29	30	

July

SUN	MON	TUE	WED	THU	FRI	SAT
						1
2	3	4	5	6	7	8
9	10	11	12	13	14	15
16	17	18	19	20	21	22
23	24	25	26	27	28	29
30						

August

SUN	MON	TUE	WED	THU	FRI	SAT
		1	2	3	4	5
6	7	8	9	10	11	12
13	14	15	16	17	18	19
20	21	22	23	24	25	26
27	28	29	30	31		

September

SUN	MON	TUE	WED	THU	FRI	SAT
					1	2
3	4	5	6	7	8	9
10	11	12	13	14	15	16
17	18	19	20	21	22	23
24	25	26	27	28	29	30

October

SUN	MON	TUE	WED	THU	FRI	SAT
1	2	3	4	5	6	7
8	9	10	11	12	13	14
15	16	17	18	19	20	21
22	23	24	25	26	27	28
29	30	31				

November

SUN	MON	TUE	WED	THU	FRI	SAT
			1	2	3	4
5	6	7	8	9	10	11
12	13	14	15	16	17	18
19	20	21	22	23	24	25
26	27	28	29	30		

December

SUN	MON	TUE	WED	THU	FRI	SAT
					1	2
3	4	5	6	7	8	9
10	11	12	13	14	15	16
17	18	19	20	21	22	23
24	25	26	27	28	29	30
31						

2024

January

SUN	MON	TUE	WED	THU	FRI	SAT
	1	2	3	4	5	6
7	8	9	10	11	12	13
14	15	16	17	18	19	20
21	22	23	24	25	26	27
28	29	30	31			

February

SUN	MON	TUE	WED	THU	FRI	SAT
				1	2	3
4	5	6	7	8	9	10
11	12	13	14	15	16	17
18	19	20	21	22	23	24
25	26	27	28	29		

March

SUN	MON	TUE	WED	THU	FRI	SAT
					1	2
3	4	5	6	7	8	9
10	11	12	13	14	15	16
17	18	19	20	21	22	23
24	25	26	27	28	29	30
31						

April

SUN	MON	TUE	WED	THU	FRI	SAT
	1	2	3	4	5	6
7	8	9	10	11	12	13
14	15	16	17	18	19	20
21	22	23	24	25	26	27
28	29	30				

May

SUN	MON	TUE	WED	THU	FRI	SAT
			1	2	3	4
5	6	7	8	9	10	11
12	13	14	15	16	17	18
19	20	21	22	23	24	25
26	27	28	29	30	31	

June

SUN	MON	TUE	WED	THU	FRI	SAT
						1
2	3	4	5	6	7	8
9	10	11	12	13	14	15
16	17	18	19	20	21	22
23	24	25	26	27	28	29
30						

July

SUN	MON	TUE	WED	THU	FRI	SAT
	1	2	3	4	5	6
7	8	9	10	11	12	13
14	15	16	17	18	19	20
21	22	23	24	25	26	27
28	29	30	31			

August

SUN	MON	TUE	WED	THU	FRI	SAT
				1	2	3
4	5	6	7	8	9	10
11	12	13	14	15	16	17
18	19	20	21	22	23	24
25	26	27	28	29	30	31

September

SUN	MON	TUE	WED	THU	FRI	SAT
1	2	3	4	5	6	7
8	9	10	11	12	13	14
15	16	17	18	19	20	21
22	23	24	25	26	27	28
29	30					

October

SUN	MON	TUE	WED	THU	FRI	SAT
		1	2	3	4	5
6	7	8	9	10	11	12
13	14	15	16	17	18	19
20	21	22	23	24	25	26
27	28	29	30	31		

November

SUN	MON	TUE	WED	THU	FRI	SAT
					1	2
3	4	5	6	7	8	9
10	11	12	13	14	15	16
17	18	19	20	21	22	23
24	25	26	27	28	29	30

December

SUN	MON	TUE	WED	THU	FRI	SAT
1	2	3	4	5	6	7
8	9	10	11	12	13	14
15	16	17	18	19	20	21
22	23	24	25	26	27	28
29	30	31				

2025

January

SUN	MON	TUE	WED	THU	FRI	SAT
			1	2	3	4
5	6	7	8	9	10	11
12	13	14	15	16	17	18
19	20	21	22	23	24	25
26	27	28	29	30	31	

February

SUN	MON	TUE	WED	THU	FRI	SAT
						1
2	3	4	5	6	7	8
9	10	11	12	13	14	15
16	17	18	19	20	21	22
23	24	25	26	27	28	

March

SUN	MON	TUE	WED	THU	FRI	SAT
						1
2	3	4	5	6	7	8
9	10	11	12	13	14	15
16	17	18	19	20	21	22
23	24	25	26	27	28	29
30	31					

April

SUN	MON	TUE	WED	THU	FRI	SAT
		1	2	3	4	5
6	7	8	9	10	11	12
13	14	15	16	17	18	19
20	21	22	23	24	25	26
27	28	29	30			

May

SUN	MON	TUE	WED	THU	FRI	SAT
				1	2	3
4	5	6	7	8	9	10
11	12	13	14	15	16	17
18	19	20	21	22	23	24
25	26	27	28	29	30	31

June

SUN	MON	TUE	WED	THU	FRI	SAT
1	2	3	4	5	6	7
8	9	10	11	12	13	14
15	16	17	18	19	20	21
22	23	24	25	26	27	28
29	30					

July

SUN	MON	TUE	WED	THU	FRI	SAT
		1	2	3	4	5
6	7	8	9	10	11	12
13	14	15	16	17	18	19
20	21	22	23	24	25	26
27	28	29	30	31		

August

SUN	MON	TUE	WED	THU	FRI	SAT
					1	2
3	4	5	6	7	8	9
10	11	12	13	14	15	16
17	18	19	20	21	22	23
24	25	26	27	28	29	30
31						

September

SUN	MON	TUE	WED	THU	FRI	SAT
	1	2	3	4	5	6
7	8	9	10	11	12	13
14	15	16	17	18	19	20
21	22	23	24	25	26	27
28	29	30				

October

SUN	MON	TUE	WED	THU	FRI	SAT
			1	2	3	4
5	6	7	8	9	10	11
12	13	14	15	16	17	18
19	20	21	22	23	24	25
26	27	28	29	30	31	

November

SUN	MON	TUE	WED	THU	FRI	SAT
						1
2	3	4	5	6	7	8
9	10	11	12	13	14	15
16	17	18	19	20	21	22
23	24	25	26	27	28	29
30						

December

SUN	MON	TUE	WED	THU	FRI	SAT
	1	2	3	4	5	6
7	8	9	10	11	12	13
14	15	16	17	18	19	20
21	22	23	24	25	26	27
28	29	30	31			

2026

January

SUN	MON	TUE	WED	THU	FRI	SAT
				1	2	3
4	5	6	7	8	9	10
11	12	13	14	15	16	17
18	19	20	21	22	23	24
25	26	27	28	29	30	31

February

SUN	MON	TUE	WED	THU	FRI	SAT
1	2	3	4	5	6	7
8	9	10	11	12	13	14
15	16	17	18	19	20	21
22	23	24	25	26	27	28

March

SUN	MON	TUE	WED	THU	FRI	SAT
1	2	3	4	5	6	7
8	9	10	11	12	13	14
15	16	17	18	19	20	21
22	23	24	25	26	27	28
29	30	31				

April

SUN	MON	TUE	WED	THU	FRI	SAT
			1	2	3	4
5	6	7	8	9	10	11
12	13	14	15	16	17	18
19	20	21	22	23	24	25
26	27	28	29	30		

May

SUN	MON	TUE	WED	THU	FRI	SAT
					1	2
3	4	5	6	7	8	9
10	11	12	13	14	15	16
17	18	19	20	21	22	23
24	25	26	27	28	29	30
31						

June

SUN	MON	TUE	WED	THU	FRI	SAT
	1	2	3	4	5	6
7	8	9	10	11	12	13
14	15	16	17	18	19	20
21	22	23	24	25	26	27
28	29	30				

July

SUN	MON	TUE	WED	THU	FRI	SAT
			1	2	3	4
5	6	7	8	9	10	11
12	13	14	15	16	17	18
19	20	21	22	23	24	25
26	27	28	29	30	31	

August

SUN	MON	TUE	WED	THU	FRI	SAT
						1
2	3	4	5	6	7	8
9	10	11	12	13	14	15
16	17	18	19	20	21	22
23	24	25	26	27	28	29
31						

September

SUN	MON	TUE	WED	THU	FRI	SAT
		1	2	3	4	5
6	7	8	9	10	11	12
13	14	15	16	17	18	19
20	21	22	23	24	25	26
27	28	29	30			

October

SUN	MON	TUE	WED	THU	FRI	SAT
				1	2	3
4	5	6	7	8	9	10
11	12	13	14	15	16	17
18	19	20	21	22	23	24
25	26	27	28	29	30	31

November

SUN	MON	TUE	WED	THU	FRI	SAT
1	2	3	4	5	6	7
8	9	10	11	12	13	14
15	16	17	18	19	20	21
22	23	24	25	26	27	28
29	30					

December

SUN	MON	TUE	WED	THU	FRI	SAT
		1	2	3	4	5
6	7	8	9	10	11	12
13	14	15	16	17	18	19
20	21	22	23	24	25	26
27	28	29	30	31		

Notes

Notes

January

Sunday	Monday	Tuesday	Wednesday
26	27	28	29
2	3	4	5
9	10	11	12
16	17	18	19
23	24	25	26
30	31	1	2

2022

Thursday	Friday	Saturday	Notes
30	31	1	
6	7	8	
13	14	15	
20	21	22	
27	28	29	
30	31	1	

February

Sunday	Monday	Tuesday	Wednesday
30	31	1	2
6	7	8	9
13	14	15	16
20	21	22	23
27	28	1	2
6	7	8	9

2022

Thursday	Friday	Saturday	Notes
3	4	5	
10	11	12	
17	18	19	
24	25	26	
31	1	2	
7	8	9	

March

Sunday	Monday	Tuesday	Wednesday
27	28	1	2
6	7	8	9
13	14	15	16
20	21	22	23
27	28	29	30
3	4	5	6

2022

Thursday	Friday	Saturday	Notes
3	4	5	
10	11	12	
17	18	19	
24	25	26	
31	1	2	
5	6	7	

April

Sunday	Monday	Tuesday	Wednesday
27	28	29	30
3	4	5	6
10	11	12	13
17	18	19	20
24	25	26	27
1	2	3	4

2022

Thursday	Friday	Saturday	Notes
31	1	2	
7	8	9	
14	15	16	
21	22	23	
28	29	30	
5	6	7	

May

Sunday	Monday	Tuesday	Wednesday
1	2	3	4
8	9	10	11
15	16	17	18
22	23	24	25
29	30	31	1
5	6	7	8

2022

Thursday	Friday	Saturday	Notes
5	6	7	
12	13	14	
19	20	21	
26	27	28	
2	3	4	
9	10	11	

June

Sunday	Monday	Tuesday	Wednesday
29	30	31	1
5	6	7	8
12	13	14	15
19	20	21	22
26	27	28	29
3	4	5	6

2022

Thursday	Friday	Saturday	Notes
2	3	4	
9	10	11	
16	17	18	
23	24	25	
30	1	2	
7	8	9	

July

Sunday	Monday	Tuesday	Wednesday
26	27	28	29
3	4	5	6
10	11	12	13
17	18	19	20
24	25	26	26
31	1	2	3

2022

Thursday	Friday	Saturday	Notes
30	1	2	
7	8	9	
14	15	16	
21	22	23	
28	29	30	
4	5	6	

August

Sunday	Monday	Tuesday	Wednesday
31	1	2	3
7	8	9	10
14	15	16	17
21	22	23	24
28	29	30	31
4	5	6	7

2022

Thursday	Friday	Saturday	Notes
4	5	6	
11	12	13	
18	19	20	
25	26	27	
1	2	3	
8	9	10	

September

Sunday	Monday	Tuesday	Wednesday
28	29	30	31
4	5	6	7
11	12	13	14
18	19	20	21
25	26	27	28
2	3	4	5

2022

Thursday	Friday	Saturday	Notes
1	2	3	
8	9	10	
15	16	17	
22	23	24	
29	30	1	
6	7	8	

October

Sunday	Monday	Tuesday	Wednesday
25	26	27	28
2	3	4	5
9	10	11	12
16	17	19	19
23	24	25	26
30	31	1	2

2022

Thursday	Friday	Saturday	Notes
29	30	1	
6	7	8	
13	14	15	
20	21	22	
27	28	29	
3	4	5	

November

Sunday	Monday	Tuesday	Wednesday
30	31	1	2
6	7	8	9
13	14	15	16
20	21	22	23
27	28	29	30
4	5	6	7

2022

Thursday	Friday	Saturday	Notes
3	4	5	
10	11	12	
17	18	19	
24	25	26	
1	2	3	
8	9	10	

December

Sunday	Monday	Tuesday	Wednesday
27	28	29	30
4	5	6	7
11	12	13	14
18	19	20	21
25	26	27	28
1	2	4	4

2022

Thursday	Friday	Saturday	Notes
1	2	3	
8	9	10	
15	16	17	
22	23	24	
29	30	31	
5	6	7	

Notes

Notes

January

Sunday	Monday	Tuesday	Wednesday
1	2	3	4
8	9	10	11
15	16	17	18
22	23	24	25
29	30	31	1
5	6	7	8

2023

Thursday	Friday	Saturday	Notes
5	6	7	
12	13	14	
19	20	21	
26	27	28	
2	3	4	
8	9	10	

February

Sunday	Monday	Tuesday	Wednesday
29	30	31	1
5	6	7	8
12	13	14	15
19	20	21	22
26	27	28	1
5	6	7	8

2023

Thursday	Friday	Saturday	Notes
2	3	4	
9	10	11	
16	17	18	
23	24	25	
2	3	4	
8	8	10	

March

Sunday	Monday	Tuesday	Wednesday
26	27	28	1
5	6	7	8
12	13	13	15
19	20	21	22
26	27	28	29
2	3	4	5

2023

Thursday	Friday	Saturday	Notes
2	3	4	
9	10	11	
16	17	18	
23	24	25	
30	31	1	
6	7	8	

April

Sunday	Monday	Tuesday	Wednesday
26	27	28	29
2	3	4	5
9	10	11	12
16	17	19	19
23	24	25	26
30	1	2	3

2023

Thursday	Friday	Saturday	Notes
30	31	1	
6	7	8	
13	14	15	
20	21	22	
27	28	29	
4	5	6	

May

Sunday	Monday	Tuesday	Wednesday
30	1	2	3
7	8	9	10
14	15	16	17
21	22	23	24
28	29	30	31
4	5	6	7

2023

Thursday	Friday	Saturday	Notes
	5	6	
11	12	13	
18	19	20	
25	26	27	
1	2	3	
8	9	10	

June

Sunday	Monday	Tuesday	Wednesday
28	29	30	31
4	5	6	7
11	12	13	14
18	19	20	21
25	26	27	28
2	3	4	5

2023

Thursday	Friday	Saturday	Notes
1	2	3	
8	9	10	
15	16	17	
22	23	24	
29	30	1	
6	7	8	

July

Sunday	Monday	Tuesday	Wednesday
25	26	27	28
2	3	4	5
9	10	11	12
16	17	18	19
23	24	25	26
30	31	1	2

2023

Thursday	Friday	Saturday	Notes
29	30	1	
6	7	8	
13	14	15	
20	21	22	
27	28	29	
3	4	5	

August

Sunday	Monday	Tuesday	Wednesday
30	31	1	2
6	7	8	9
13	14	15	16
20	21	22	23
27	28	29	30
3	4	5	6

2023

Thursday	Friday	Saturday	Notes
3	4	5	
10	11	12	
17	18	19	
24	25	26	
31	1	2	
7	8	9	

September

Sunday	Monday	Tuesday	Wednesday
27	28	29	30
3	4	5	6
10	11	12	13
17	18	19	20
24	25	26	27
1	2	3	4

2023

Thursday	Friday	Saturday	Notes
31	1	2	
7	8	9	
14	15	16	
21	22	23	
28	29	30	
5	6	6	

October

Sunday	Monday	Tuesday	Wednesday
1	2	3	4
8	9	10	11
15	16	17	18
22	23	24	25
29	30	31	1
5	6	7	8

2023

Thursday	Friday	Saturday	Notes
5	6	7	
12	13	14	
19	20	21	
26	27	28	
2	3	4	
9	10	11	

November

Sunday	Monday	Tuesday	Wednesday
29	30	31	1
5	6	7	8
12	13	14	15
19	20	21	22
26	27	28	29
3	4	5	6

2023

Thursday	Friday	Saturday	Notes
2	3	4	
9	10	11	
16	17	18	
23	24	25	
30	1	2	
7	8	9	

December

Sunday	Monday	Tuesday	Wednesday
26	27	28	29
3	4	5	6
10	11	12	13
18	19	20	21
24	25	26	27
31	1	2	3

2023

Thursday	Friday	Saturday	Notes
30	1	2	
7	8	9	
14	15	16	
21	22	23	
28	29	30	
4	5	6	

Notes

Notes

January

Sunday	Monday	Tuesday	Wednesday
31	1	2	3
7	8	9	10
14	15	16	17
21	22	23	24
28	29	30	31
4	5	6	7

2024

Thursday	Friday	Saturday	Notes
4	5	6	
11	12	13	
18	19	20	
25	26	27	
1	2	3	
8	9	10	

February

Sunday	Monday	Tuesday	Wednesday
28	29	30	31
4	5	6	7
11	12	13	14
18	19	20	21
25	26	27	28
3	4	5	6

2024

Thursday	Friday	Saturday	Notes
1	2	3	
8	9	10	
15	16	17	
22	23	24	
29	1	2	
7	8	9	

March

Sunday	Monday	Tuesday	Wednesday
25	26	27	28
3	4	5	6
10	11	12	13
17	18	19	20
24	25	26	27
31	1	2	3

2024

Thursday	Friday	Saturday	Notes
29	1	2	
7	8	9	
14	15	16	
21	22	23	
28	29	30	
4	5	6	

April

Sunday	Monday	Tuesday	Wednesday
31	1	2	3
7	8	9	10
14	15	16	17
21	22	23	24
28	29	30	1
5	6	7	8

2024

Thursday	Friday	Saturday	Notes
4	5	6	
11	12	13	
18	19	20	
25	26	27	
2	3	4	
9	10	11	

May

Sunday	Monday	Tuesday	Wednesday
28	29	30	1
5	6	7	8
12	13	14	15
19	20	21	22
26	27	28	29
2	3	4	5

2024

Thursday	Friday	Saturday	Notes
2	3	4	
9	10	11	
16	17	18	
23	24	25	
30	31	1	
6	7	8	

June

Sunday	Monday	Tuesday	Wednesday
26	27	28	29
2	3	4	5
9	10	11	12
16	17	18	19
23	24	25	26
30	1	2	3

2024

Thursday	Friday	Saturday	Notes
30	31	1	
6	7	8	
13	14	15	
20	21	22	
27	28	29	
4	5	6	

July

Sunday	Monday	Tuesday	Wednesday
30	1	2	3
7	8	9	10
14	15	16	17
21	22	23	24
28	29	30	31
4	5	6	7

2024

Thursday	Friday	Saturday	Notes
4	5	6	
11	12	13	
18	19	20	
25	26	27	
1	2	3	
8	9	10	

August

Sunday	Monday	Tuesday	Wednesday
28	29	30	31
4	5	6	7
11	12	13	14
18	19	20	21
25	26	27	28
1	2	3	4

2024

Thursday	Friday	Saturday	Notes
1	2	3	
8	9	10	
15	16	17	
22	23	24	
29	30	31	
5	6	7	

September

Sunday	Monday	Tuesday	Wednesday
1	2	3	4
8	9	10	11
15	16	17	18
22	23	24	25
29	30	1	2
6	7	8	9

2024

Thursday	Friday	Saturday	Notes
5	6	7	
12	13	14	
19	20	21	
26	27	28	
3	4	5	
10	11	12	

October

Sunday	Monday	Tuesday	Wednesday
29	30	1	2
6	7	8	9
12	13	14	15
19	20	21	22
26	27	28	29
3	4	5	6

2024

Thursday	Friday	Saturday	Notes
3	4	5	
10	11	12	
17	18	19	
24	25	26	
31	1	2	
7	8	9	

November

Sunday	Monday	Tuesday	Wednesday
27	28	29	30
3	4	5	6
10	11	12	13
17	18	19	20
24	25	26	27
1	2	3	4

2024

Thursday	Friday	Saturday	Notes
31	1	2	
7	8	9	
14	15	16	
21	22	23	
28	29	30	
5	6	7	

December

Sunday	Monday	Tuesday	Wednesday
1	2	3	4
8	9	10	11
15	16	17	18
22	23	24	25
29	30	31	1
5	6	7	8

2024

Thursday	Friday	Saturday	Notes
6	7	8	
12	13	14	
19	20	21	
26	27	28	
2	3	4	
9	10	11	

Notes

Notes

January

Sunday	Monday	Tuesday	Wednesday
29	30	31	1
5	6	7	8
12	13	14	15
19	20	21	22
26	27	28	29
2	3	4	5

2025

Thursday	Friday	Saturday	Notes
2	3	4	
9	10	11	
16	17	18	
23	24	25	
30	31	1	
6	7	8	

February

Sunday	Monday	Tuesday	Wednesday
26	27	28	29
2	3	4	5
9	10	11	12
16	17	18	19
23	24	25	26
2	3	4	5

2025

Thursday	Friday	Saturday	Notes
30	31	1	
6	7	8	
13	14	15	
20	21	22	
27	28	1	
6	7	8	

March

Sunday	Monday	Tuesday	Wednesday
23	24	25	26
2	3	4	5
9	10	11	12
16	17	18	19
23	24	25	26
30	31	1	2

2025

Thursday	Friday	Saturday	Notes
27	28	1	
6	7	8	
13	14	15	
20	21	22	
27	28	29	
3	4	5	

April

Sunday	Monday	Tuesday	Wednesday
30	31	1	2
6	7	8	9
13	14	15	16
20	21	22	23
27	28	29	30
4	5	6	7

2025

Thursday	Friday	Saturday	Notes
3	4	5	
10	11	12	
17	18	19	
24	25	26	
1	2	3	
8	9	10	

May

Sunday	Monday	Tuesday	Wednesday
27	28	29	30
4	5	6	7
11	12	13	14
18	19	20	21
25	26	27	28
1	2	3	4

2025

Thursday	Friday	Saturday	Notes
1	2	3	
8	9	10	
15	16	17	
22	23	24	
29	30	31	
5	6	7	

June

Sunday	Monday	Tuesday	Wednesday
1	2	3	4
8	9	10	11
15	16	17	18
22	23	24	25
29	30	1	2
6	7	8	9

2025

Thursday	Friday	Saturday	Notes
5	6	7	
12	13	14	
19	20	21	
26	27	28	
3	4	5	
10	11	12	

July

Sunday	Monday	Tuesday	Wednesday
29	30	1	2
6	7	8	9
13	14	15	16
20	21	22	23
27	28	29	30
3	4	5	6

2025

Thursday	Friday	Saturday	Notes
3	4	5	
10	11	12	
17	18	19	
24	25	26	
31	1	2	
7	8	9	

August

Sunday	Monday	Tuesday	Wednesday
27	28	29	30
3	4	5	6
10	11	12	13
17	18	19	20
24	25	26	27
31	1	2	3

2025

Thursday	Friday	Saturday	Notes
31	1	2	
7	8	9	
14	15	16	
21	22	23	
28	29	30	
4	5	5	

September

Sunday	Monday	Tuesday	Wednesday
31	1	2	3
7	8	9	10
14	15	16	17
21	22	23	24
28	29	30	1
5	6	7	8

2025

Thursday	Friday	Saturday	Notes
4	5	6	
11	12	13	
18	19	20	
25	26	27	
2	3	4	
9	10	11	

October

Sunday	Monday	Tuesday	Wednesday
28	29	30	1
5	6	7	8
12	13	14	15
19	20	21	22
26	27	28	29
2	3	4	5

2025

Thursday	Friday	Saturday	Notes
2	3	4	
9	10	11	
16	17	18	
13	24	25	
30	31	1	
6	7	8	

November

Sunday	Monday	Tuesday	Wednesday
26	27	28	29
2	3	4	5
9	10	11	12
16	17	18	19
23	24	25	26
30	1	2	3

2025

Thursday	Friday	Saturday	Notes
30	31	1	
6	7	8	
13	14	15	
20	21	22	
27	28	29	
4	5	6	

December

Sunday	Monday	Tuesday	Wednesday
30	1	2	3
7	8	9	10
14	15	16	17
21	22	23	24
28	29	30	31
4	5	6	7

2025

Thursday	Friday	Saturday	Notes
4	5	6	
11	12	13	
18	19	20	
25	26	27	
1	2	3	
8	9	10	

Notes

Notes

January

Sunday	Monday	Tuesday	Wednesday
28	29	30	31
4	5	6	7
11	12	13	14
18	19	20	21
25	26	27	28
1	2	3	4

2026

Thursday	Friday	Saturday	Notes
1	2	3	
8	9	10	
15	16	17	
22	23	24	
29	30	31	
5	6	7	

February

Sunday	Monday	Tuesday	Wednesday
1	2	3	4
8	9	10	11
15	16	17	18
22	23	24	25
1	2	3	4
8	9	10	11

2026

Thursday	Friday	Saturday	Notes
5	6	7	
12	13	14	
19	20	21	
26	27	28	
5	6	7	
12	13	14	

March

Sunday	Monday	Tuesday	Wednesday
1	2	3	4
8	9	10	11
15	16	17	18
22	23	24	25
29	30	31	1
5	6	7	8

2026

Thursday	Friday	Saturday	Notes
5	6	7	
12	13	14	
19	20	21	
26	27	28	
2	3	4	
9	10	11	

April

Sunday	Monday	Tuesday	Wednesday
29	30	31	1
5	6	7	8
12	13	14	15
19	20	21	22
26	27	28	29
3	4	5	6

2026

Thursday	Friday	Saturday	Notes
2	3	4	
9	10	11	
16	17	18	
23	24	25	
30	1	2	
7	8	9	

May

Sunday	Monday	Tuesday	Wednesday
26	27	28	29
3	4	5	6
10	11	12	13
17	18	19	20
24	25	26	27
31	1	2	3

2026

Thursday	Friday	Saturday	Notes
30	1	2	
7	8	9	
14	15	16	
21	22	23	
28	29	30	
4	5	6	

June

Sunday	Monday	Tuesday	Wednesday
31	1	2	3
7	8	9	10
14	15	16	17
21	22	23	24
28	29	30	1
5	6	7	8

2026

Thursday	Friday	Saturday	Notes
4	5	6	
11	12	13	
18	19	20	
25	26	27	
2	3	4	
9	10	11	

July

Sunday	Monday	Tuesday	Wednesday
28	29	30	1
5	6	7	8
12	13	14	15
19	20	21	22
26	27	28	29
2	3	4	5

2026

Thursday	Friday	Saturday	Notes
3	3	4	
9	10	11	
16	17	18	
23	24	25	
30	31	1	
6	7	8	

August

Sunday	Monday	Tuesday	Wednesday
26	27	28	29
2	3	4	5
9	10	11	12
16	17	18	19
23	24	25	26
30	31	1	2

2026

Thursday	Friday	Saturday	Notes
30	31	1	
6	7	8	
13	14	15	
20	21	22	
27	28	29	
3	4	5	

September

Sunday	Monday	Tuesday	Wednesday
30	31	1	2
6	7	8	9
13	14	15	16
20	21	22	23
27	28	29	30
27	28	29	30

2026

Thursday	Friday	Saturday	Notes
3	4	5	
10	11	12	
17	18	19	
24	25	26	
1	2	3	
8	9	10	

October

Sunday	Monday	Tuesday	Wednesday
27	28	29	30
4	5	6	7
11	12	13	14
18	19	20	21
25	26	27	28
1	2	3	4

2026

Thursday	Friday	Saturday	Notes
1	2	3	
8	9	10	
15	16	17	
22	23	24	
29	30	31	
5	6	7	

November

Sunday	Monday	Tuesday	Wednesday
1	2	3	4
8	9	10	11
15	16	17	18
22	23	24	25
29	30	1	2
6	7	8	9

2026

Thursday	Friday	Saturday	Notes
5	6	7	
12	13	14	
19	20	21	
26	27	28	
3	4	5	
10	11	12	

December

Sunday	Monday	Tuesday	Wednesday
29	30	1	2
6	7	8	9
13	14	15	16
20	21	22	23
27	28	29	30
3	4	5	6

2026

Thursday	Friday	Saturday	Notes
3	4	5	
10	11	12	
17	18	19	
24	25	26	
31	1	2	
7	8	9	

Notes

Notes

Passwords

Website:
Username:
Password:
Password:
PW Hint:

Website:
Username:
Password:
Password:
PW Hint:

Website:
Username:
Password:
Password:
PW Hint:

Website:
Username:
Password:
Password:
PW Hint:

Website:
Username:
Password:
Password:
PW Hint:

Passwords

Website:
Username:
Password:
Password:
PW Hint:

Website:
Username:
Password:
Password:
PW Hint:

Website:
Username:
Password:
Password:
PW Hint:

Website:
Username:
Password:
Password:
PW Hint:

Website:
Username:
Password:
Password:
PW Hint:

Passwords

Website:

Username:

Password:

Password:

PW Hint:

Website:

Username:

Password:

Password:

PW Hint:

Website:

Username:

Password:

Password:

PW Hint:

Website:

Username:

Password:

Password:

PW Hint:

Website:

Username:

Password:

Password:

PW Hint:

Passwords

Website:
Username:
Password:
Password:
PW Hint:

Website:
Username:
Password:
Password:
PW Hint:

Website:
Username:
Password:
Password:
PW Hint:

Website:
Username:
Password:
Password:
PW Hint:

Website:
Username:
Password:
Password:
PW Hint:

Passwords

Website:
Username:
Password:
Password:
PW Hint:

Website:
Username:
Password:
Password:
PW Hint:

Website:
Username:
Password:
Password:
PW Hint:

Website:
Username:
Password:
Password:
PW Hint:

Website:
Username:
Password:
Password:
PW Hint:

Passwords

Website:
Username:
Password:
Password:
PW Hint:

Website:
Username:
Password:
Password:
PW Hint:

Website:
Username:
Password:
Password:
PW Hint:

Website:
Username:
Password:
Password:
PW Hint:

Website:
Username:
Password:
Password:
PW Hint:

Passwords

Website:
Username:
Password:
Password:
PW Hint:

Website:
Username:
Password:
Password:
PW Hint:

Website:
Username:
Password:
Password:
PW Hint:

Website:
Username:
Password:
Password:
PW Hint:

Website:
Username:
Password:
Password:
PW Hint:

Passwords

Website:

Username:

Password:

Password:

PW Hint:

Website:

Username:

Password:

Password:

PW Hint:

Website:

Username:

Password:

Password:

PW Hint:

Website:

Username:

Password:

Password:

PW Hint:

Website:

Username:

Password:

Password:

PW Hint:

Contact Information

Name:
Business:
Website
Email:
Phone:
Notes:

Name:
Business:
Website
Email:
Phone:
Notes:

Name:
Business:
Website
Email:
Phone:
Notes:

Name:
Business:
Website
Email:
Phone:
Notes:

Name:
Business:
Website
Email:
Phone:
Notes:

Contact Information

Name:
Business:
Website
Email:
Phone:
Notes:

Name:
Business:
Website
Email:
Phone:
Notes:

Name:
Business:
Website
Email:
Phone:
Notes:

Name:
Business:
Website
Email:
Phone:
Notes:

Name:
Business:
Website
Email:
Phone:
Notes:

Contact Information

Name:
Business:
Website
Email:
Phone:
Notes:

Name:
Business:
Website
Email:
Phone:
Notes:

Name:
Business:
Website
Email:
Phone:
Notes:

Name:
Business:
Website
Email:
Phone:
Notes:

Name:
Business:
Website
Email:
Phone:
Notes:

Contact Information

Name:
Business:
Website
Email:
Phone:
Notes:

Name:
Business:
Website
Email:
Phone:
Notes:

Name:
Business:
Website
Email:
Phone:
Notes:

Name:
Business:
Website
Email:
Phone:
Notes:

Name:
Business:
Website
Email:
Phone:
Notes:

Contact Information

Name:
Business:
Website
Email:
Phone:
Notes:

Name:
Business:
Website
Email:
Phone:
Notes:

Name:
Business:
Website
Email:
Phone:
Notes:

Name:
Business:
Website
Email:
Phone:
Notes:

Name:
Business:
Website
Email:
Phone:
Notes:

Contact Information

Name:
Business:
Website
Email:
Phone:
Notes:

Name:
Business:
Website
Email:
Phone:
Notes:

Name:
Business:
Website
Email:
Phone:
Notes:

Name:
Business:
Website
Email:
Phone:
Notes:

Name:
Business:
Website
Email:
Phone:
Notes:

Notes

Notes

Made in United States
Orlando, FL
12 October 2023

37825237R00087